Properties of Materials

Heavy or Light

Charlotte Guillain

Heinemann
LIBRARY

www.heinemannlibrary.co.uk
Visit our website to find out more information about Heinemann Library books.

To order:
☎ Phone +44 (0) 1865 888066
🖷 Fax +44 (0) 1865 314091
💻 Visit www.heinemannlibrary.co.uk

Heinemann is an imprint of Capstone Global Library Limited, a company incorporated in England and Wales having its registered office at 7 Pilgrim Street, London, EC4V 6LB – Registered company number: 6695582

Edited by Charlotte Guillain and Catherine Veitch
Designed by Joanna Hinton-Malivoire
Picture research by Elizabeth Alexander
Originated by Heinemann Library
Printed by South China Printing Company Limited

ISBN 978 0 431 19347 2 (hardback)
13 12 11 10 09
10 9 8 7 6 5 4 3 2 1

British Library Cataloguing in Publication Data
Guillain, Charlotte
Heavy or light. – (Properties of materials)
530.8'1
A full catalogue record for this book is available from the British Library.

Acknowledgements
The author and publishers are grateful to the following for permission to reproduce copyright material:
Alamy pp. **9** (© mediablitzimages (UK) Limited), **19** (© Jupiterimages/Creatas); © Capstone Publishers p. **22** main (Karon Dubke); Getty Images pp. **8** (Jamie Grill/Iconica), **10** (Betsie Van der Meer/Stone+), **13**, **23** middle (Dorling Kindersley), **17** (Tim Hall/Taxi); Photolibrary pp. **5** (David Stover/Imagestate), **6** (Jonathan Kirn), **7**, **23** bottom (Luis Padilla/age footstock), **12**, **23** top (ColorBlind Images/Blend Images), **14** (Philip Laurell), **18** (© FRUMM John/Hemis); Shutterstock pp. **4** (© Dainis Derics), **11** (© Hallgerd), **15** (© Jaimie Duplass), **16** (© mates), **20** (© prism_68), **21** (© Brian A. Jackson), **22** middle bottom (© anacarol).

Cover photograph of a kite reproduced with permission of istockphoto (© Piotr Sikora). Back cover photograph of dandelion seeds reproduced with permission of Shutterstock (© Brian A. Jackson).

The publishers would like to thank Nancy Harris and Adriana Scalise for their assistance in the preparation of this book.

Every effort has been made to contact copyright holders of any material reproduced in this book. Any omissions will be rectified in subsequent printings if notice is given to the publisher.

Contents

Heavy materials

Some things are heavy.

Heavy things are hard to lift.

Heavy things weigh a lot.

Heavy things can be solid.

Light materials

Some things are light.

Light things are easy to lift.

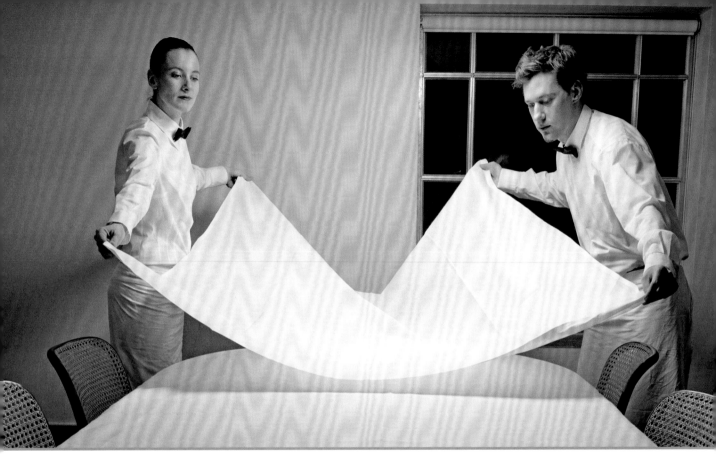

Light things do not weigh a lot.

Light things can be soft.

Heavy and light materials

A metal car is heavy. It is hard to lift.

Metal foil is light. It is easy to lift.

A tree trunk is heavy.
It is hard to lift.

A twig is light.
It is easy to lift.

You can tell if something is heavy
or light.

You can feel if something is heavy or light.

Heavy things are hard to move.

Light things are easy to move.

Sometimes things look heavy.

Sometimes things look light.

Quiz

Which things look heavy?
Which things look light?

Picture glossary

metal hard, shiny material

metal foil very thin sheets of metal. Foil is often used to wrap food.

solid fixed shape that is not a gas or a liquid

Index

Note to parents and teachers
Before reading
Tell children that some materials are heavy and some are light. Heavy materials are hard to lift and light materials are easy to lift. In partners, ask children to brainstorm heavy and light materials. Give children two minutes to turn and talk to a partner. When they are finished, ask the children to share examples and create a chart with two columns – heavy objects and light objects.

After reading
Give children a clipboard, pencil, and piece of paper with two columns – heavy objects and light objects. Tell the children that they are going to go on a hunt around the classroom for heavy and light objects. Put the children into small groups. Children can draw or write the objects they see in the appropriate columns. Give them 15 minutes. When the hunt is done, ask the children the following questions:
1.　　"What objects did you find?"
2.　　"Which object is the heaviest?"
3.　　"Which object is the lightest?"